BLACK VOICES ON RACE
DUKE ELLINGTON

by Chyina Powell

T0014698

FOCUS
READERS®

NAVIGATOR

WWW.FOCUSREADERS.COM

Focus Readers is distributed by North Star Editions:
sales@northstareditions.com | 888-417-0195

Produced for Focus Readers by Red Line Editorial.

Content Consultant: James Gordon Williams, PhD, Associate Professor of Music in African American Studies, Syracuse University

Photographs ©: Pictorial Press Ltd./Alamy, cover, 1, 15; Chyina Powell, 2; Gordon Parks/Library of Congress, 4–5; A.F. Archive/Alamy, 7; Mirror Pix/Newscom, 8–9; Imago History Collection/Alamy, 11; Charlotte Brooks/Library of Congress, 12–13, 19, 20–21; AP Images, 17; Klaus Frings/AP Images, 22; Red Line Editorial, 25; John Lent/AP Images, 26–27; John Duricka/AP Images, 29

Library of Congress Cataloging-in-Publication Data
Names: Powell, Chyina, author.
Title: Duke Ellington / by Chyina Powell.
Description: Lake Elmo, MN : Focus Readers, [2023] | Series: Black voices on race | Includes index. | Audience: Grades 4-6
Identifiers: LCCN 2022008179 (print) | LCCN 2022008180 (ebook) | ISBN 9781637392621 (hardcover) | ISBN 9781637393147 (paperback) | ISBN 9781637394144 (pdf) | ISBN 9781637393666 (ebook)
Subjects: LCSH: Ellington, Duke, 1899-1974--Juvenile literature. | Composers--United States--Biography--Juvenile literature. | Band directors--United States--Biography--Juvenile literature. | Jazz musicians--United States--Biography--Juvenile literature. | African American musicians--Juvenile literature. | Music and race--United States--History--20th century--Juvenile literature.
Classification: LCC ML3930.E44 P68 2023 (print) | LCC ML3930.E44 (ebook) | DDC 781.65092 [B]--dc23
LC record available at https://lccn.loc.gov/2022008179
LC ebook record available at https://lccn.loc.gov/2022008180

Printed in the United States of America
Mankato, MN
082022

ABOUT THE AUTHOR

Chyina Powell is a freelance writer and editor. She is the founder of both Powell Editorial and the Women of Color Writers' Circle and can often be found with a cup of tea and a book in her hand.

TABLE OF CONTENTS

CHAPTER 1

A MAN AND HIS MUSIC

On January 23, 1943, Duke Ellington went onstage at Carnegie Hall. He stood before a huge crowd. He looked professional with his fancy suit. Through his elegant appearance, he broke **stereotypes** about what a Black man should look like. He was ready to use music to say even more about racism.

Duke Ellington performed at the historic Carnegie Hall more than 20 times during his career.

Ellington began conducting a jazz piece he'd written. "Black, Brown and Beige" started with the sound of drums. The opening shared the horrors of slavery. The middle told the struggles of Black people in post-slavery America. The ending represented the current complexity of Black life. This piece paved the way for protest music.

During his long career, Ellington wrote more than 2,000 songs. He performed before white and Black audiences. He was beloved by working-class and famous people. He toured Europe, Asia, North America, and South America. Ellington's music was heard all around

Ellington later expanded "Black, Brown and Beige" in 1958.

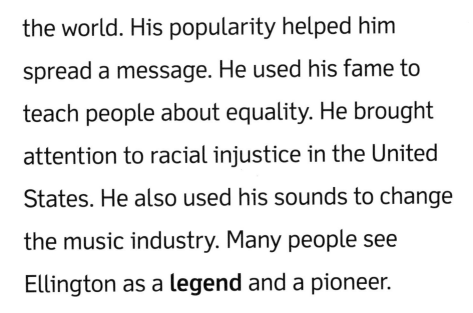

the world. His popularity helped him spread a message. He used his fame to teach people about equality. He brought attention to racial injustice in the United States. He also used his sounds to change the music industry. Many people see Ellington as a **legend** and a pioneer.

CHAPTER 2

GROWING UP MUSICAL

Edward Kennedy Ellington was born on April 29, 1899, in Washington, DC. Both of his parents were pianists. Edward's father played songs from operas. His mother played popular music. Edward was seven years old when he began studying music. He enjoyed the lessons.

Edward Ellington wrote his first song before he could even read music.

As a teenager, Edward wrote his first song. It was called "Soda Fountain Rag." He wrote it in the styles of his favorite musicians, such as James P. Johnson and Luckey Roberts. Edward never recorded this piece. But his interest in music grew.

THE DUKE

Edward Ellington was raised in a middle-class family. His father worked in the White House. His mother valued manners and grace. They taught him how to be a gentleman. By age seven, Edward's fine manners made him seem like royalty. They earned him the nickname "Duke." When Edward began to play professionally, he used his nickname. He was known as Duke Ellington for his performances.

During Edward's childhood, Black people made up 31 percent of the population in Washington, DC.

Meanwhile, Edward went to a **segregated** school. There, he learned Black history. He learned to be proud of being Black. He also learned to fight injustice through personal success.

Soon, Edward began playing piano at parties and clubs. It was a fun job. So, he decided to make music for a living. He saw musical success as a way to spread a message about race.

CHAPTER 3

THE MAKING OF A MUSICIAN

At age 18, Duke Ellington became the bandleader of his first musical group. A bandleader instructs others while playing with them. He creates the songs and runs practices. He also shapes the sound of the band. Ellington's first group was small. They played jazz and ragtime in Washington, DC.

Duke Ellington (center) led many bands and orchestras of skillful jazz musicians.

Ellington moved to New York City at age 24. He wanted to make a name for himself in the music industry. But racism was a challenge. Black Americans faced **discrimination**. This unfair treatment

ALL ABOUT JAZZ

Duke Ellington was seen as a great jazz leader. Black Americans created jazz in the late 1800s and early 1900s. Jazz uses European musical elements. But it is inspired by Black Americans' complex experiences in America. Jazz grew out of other forms of music, such as ragtime and blues. It is a very personal type of music. Because jazz is based on self-expression, improvisation is important. This means creating music in the moment. Good improvising requires years of study and practice.

Black audiences were not allowed in the Cotton Club.

was both normal and legal. For example, Ellington's band became the main band for the Cotton Club in 1927. This famous club was segregated. White audiences listened to Black performers. But the performers could enter only through back doors.

Ellington's time at the Cotton Club made him famous. His band performed as the Cotton Club's main band for approximately three years. During this time, Ellington brought together key musicians for his band. Many of them were important jazz artists on their own. Jazz musicians take pride in their own sounds. If the same song is played by different artists, it will not sound the same. Ellington used this to his benefit. He used his musicians' differences to inspire new sounds.

Soon, Ellington's small band grew into a big band. In jazz, a big band has 4 sections and 10 musicians or more.

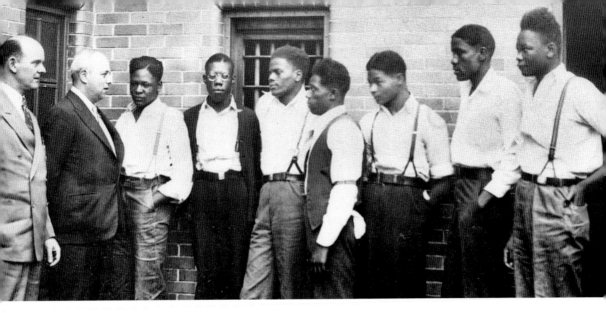

Ellington held benefit concerts for the Scottsboro Boys. In 1931, they were imprisoned for a crime they didn't do.

Ellington's original band grew to 14 members.

Ellington used his growing fame to support Black rights. For example, he supported the National Association for the Advancement of Colored People. This organization works for racial equality. Ellington also held concerts to raise money for important causes.

MUSIC AND THE BLACK EXPERIENCE

Until the 1960s, racial discrimination was legal in the United States. Segregation kept Black and white people apart. Black people struggled to have their basic human rights recognized.

At the same time, Black music thrived. Duke Ellington saw music as a way to raise awareness. Through music, he brought attention to the Black experience in America. He said, "What we could not say openly, we expressed in music."[1] Music allowed Black people the freedom of self-expression. They shared their thoughts, feelings, and ideas through music.

Ellington also saw Black music as a form of **activism**. He said, "You can say anything you want on the trombone, but you gotta be careful with

Duke Ellington and his band often had to stay in segregated hotels as they toured in the South.

words."[2] He meant that white people might not listen to Black activists. But they might listen to Black music. White audiences had long listened to jazz. Ellington became popular as a jazz leader. He used his musical success to challenge racist ideas about Black people.

1. Laura Townsend. "How Duke Ellington Used His Appearance to Subvert Racist Stereotypes, and Other Ways He Fought Racism." *PBS.* Accessed February 4, 2022. www.pbs.org/wnet/americanmasters.
2. Ibid.

CHAPTER 4

A TRUE GENIUS

It wasn't long before Duke Ellington became a jazz legend. He wrote thousands of **compositions**. He wrote music to fit his band members' talents. Ellington worked with great musicians such as trumpeter Louis Armstrong and singer Ella Fitzgerald. He composed music for films and appeared in them.

A composer writes original music. An arranger takes others' music and interprets it in a new way. Duke Ellington was an expert in both roles.

Ellington (second from left) used the word "Black" in many of his song titles to draw attention to Black life.

And he blended different forms of music to make new sounds. All of these activities earned him respect from music critics.

Ellington never lost his focus on Black rights. He believed in social justice. He thought everyone should be treated equally. In 1941, he wrote a musical to fight prejudice. *Jump for Joy* celebrated the Black race. It included singing, dancing, and even comedy. The goal

THE SWING ERA

Duke Ellington did not like the term *jazz*, because it was connected to racist ideas about Black people. Instead, he defined his music as beyond category. He explored his own style. As part of this exploration, he helped invent swing music. Swing is rooted in Black American culture. It is known for its **rhythm**. It emphasizes beats 2 and 4. And it inspires people to dance. As swing became popular, new dances arose. The Lindy Hop and the jitterbug are two examples.

of the musical was to feature Black intelligence and support equality.

Ellington wanted to change the ideas white people had about Black people. At the time, many films and plays showed Black people as servants or clowns. Ellington challenged these racist stereotypes. He used his music to highlight Black genius.

Ellington also fought segregation. By 1961, he began refusing to play for segregated crowds. Black and white audience members had to sit together when he performed.

Ellington and his band soon became popular around the world. They even served as jazz **ambassadors** during the **Cold War** (1947–1989). The US government sent them to perform worldwide. The band continued to experience racism at home. Yet the government used them to represent American democracy and culture abroad.

SELECTED PIECES

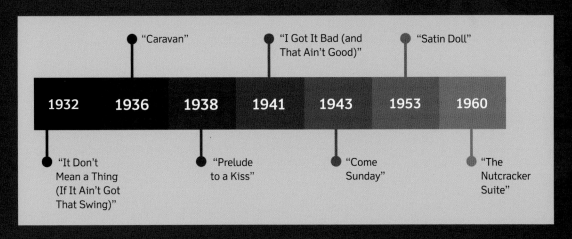

- "Caravan" (1936)
- "I Got It Bad (and That Ain't Good)" (1941)
- "Satin Doll" (1953)

1932 — **1936** — **1938** — **1941** — **1943** — **1953** — **1960**

- "It Don't Mean a Thing (If It Ain't Got That Swing)" (1932)
- "Prelude to a Kiss" (1938)
- "Come Sunday" (1943)
- "The Nutcracker Suite" (1960)

CHAPTER 5

ELLINGTON'S LEGACY

Duke Ellington's career lasted more than 50 years. During that time, Ellington won several awards because of his musical talents. In total, he won 11 Grammy Awards. He also received the Presidential Medal of Freedom in 1969. This award is the highest honor a US civilian can receive.

Duke Ellington won two Grammy Awards at the 1968 ceremony.

Later, Ellington wrote a book about his life. *Music Is My Mistress* was published in 1973. It focused on how he used music to express himself. The book mentioned how Ellington wanted to be seen as an artist. He believed race should not matter when it came to the arts.

Ellington died of lung cancer on May 24, 1974. He led his band up until his death. People continued to celebrate Ellington after his death. For example, he received the Pulitzer Prize in 1999. The prize honored Ellington's entire life and career.

Duke Ellington changed music forever. His music also helped inspire a belief in

Ellington has an unofficial holiday. Duke Ellington Day is celebrated on April 29, which was his birthday.

social justice all over the world. His final words summed up his life: "Music is how I live, why I live, and how I will be remembered."[3] Ellington's music is still loved and remembered today.

3. "Duke Ellington." *Biography.com*. Accessed February 4, 2022. www.biography.com/musician/duke-ellington.

FOCUS ON
DUKE ELLINGTON

Write your answers on a separate piece of paper.

1. Write a paragraph that describes the main ideas of Chapter 4.

2. If you were to blend different forms of music as Duke Ellington did, which forms would you blend? Why?

3. When did Ellington stop playing for segregated crowds?

   A. 1927
   B. 1941
   C. 1961

4. How might jazz be seen as a form of self-expression?

   A. Jazz involves improvisation, so musicians create the music in the moment based on how they're feeling.
   B. Jazz involves many musicians playing together, so individual musicians cannot be heard.
   C. Jazz involves dancing, so musicians can show off their skills.

Answer key on page 32.

GLOSSARY

activism
Actions to make social or political changes.

ambassadors
Official representatives of a country.

Cold War
A conflict of ideals between the United States and the Soviet Union that took place from 1947 to 1989.

compositions
Pieces of music written for voices or instruments.

discrimination
Unfair treatment of others based on who they are or how they look.

legend
Someone known and admired for skill in a certain area.

rhythm
In music, the mix of short and long sounds to create patterns.

segregated
Separate or set apart based on race, gender, or religion.

stereotypes
Overly simple and harmful ideas of how all members of a certain group are.

TO LEARN MORE

BOOKS

Celenza, Anna Harwell. *Duke Ellington's Nutcracker Suite*. Watertown, MA: Charlesbridge, 2018.

Harris, Duchess, and Martha London. *The Harlem Renaissance*. Minneapolis: Abdo Publishing, 2020.

Payne, M. D. *Who Was Duke Ellington?* New York: Penguin Workshop, 2020.

NOTE TO EDUCATORS

Visit **www.focusreaders.com** to find lesson plans, activities, links, and other resources related to this title.

INDEX

Answer Key: 1. Answers will vary; 2. Answers will vary; 3. C; 4. A